WAITING

A BOOK OF POEMS

BY

NASREEN PEJVACK

Nasreen Pejvack

Copyright © Nasreen Pejvack 2018

Except for the use of short passages for review purposes, no part of this book may be reproduced, in pat or in whole, or transmitted in any form or by any means, electronically or mechanically, including photocopying, recording, or any information or storage retrieval system, without prior permission in writing from the Author.

Author: Nasreen Pejvack
Cover Design: Nasreen Pejvack

Website: http://examine-consider-act.ca
info@examine-consider-act.ca

ISBN: 978-1-7753223-1-3 (Paperback)
ISBN: 978-1-7753223-3-7 (eBook)

Paperback available at McNally Robinson Booksellers, and online at Amazon.com

McNally Robinson Booksellers
1120 Grant Avenue, Winnipeg, MB Canada R3M 2A6
Toll Free 1-800-561-1833

http://www.mcnallyrobinson.com/home

CONTENTS

1. Author Forward v
2. Howling For Life 8
3. Waiting 14
4. Faces of War 16
5. Eternal Remembrance Day 22
6. Beyond Control 24
7. Remembering Spartacus 26
8. Law of the Jungle 29
9. One Unified Earth 31
10. Women 33
11. Love and Inspiration 41
12. I Choose 43
13. Intelligent Species 45
14. My Garden, My Sanctuary 48
15. Spring Always Arrives 49
16. In a Day 51
17. Sparrow 53
18. Share 55
19. Dew 56
20. I Do Talk of Love! 58
21. I Love a Man 60
22. My Other Half 62

23.	Delineate Love	64
24.	Acknowledgment	72
25.	Author Biography	73

Author Forward

If I believe my Country is the planet Earth, then my loyalties lie there. I was born in the Middle-Eastern region, in the province of Iran, in the city of Tehran. Throughout much of my adulthood, I have been on the north side of my country Earth, in the province of Canada, living in Ottawa and Vancouver. I have also lived in other jurisdictions of this blue/green country, such as Greece and America, and in each I have learned much from its people and its culture.

In my childhood I thought that religion meant peace. I heard and read the representatives of each religion preach kindness and a better life for all. However, as I matured, I saw that they had lied. Religions killed many to convert others, or punished those of their own who did not obey. So, my own belief developed into a simple love for humanity, and for this planet as my country, and for all life that accompanies us here.

This collection of poems reflects my life's learning and experiences from the time I was old enough to know my surroundings; old enough to understand and painfully observe indifferent people and their competitive, egotistically greedy nature.

This disposition leads us astray, for instance into pretending uncertainty about climate change, as if scientists haven't confirmed the effects of pumping greenhouse gases and other chemicals into our air, land and water. The issue certainly gets lots of press.

Yet I haven't heard nearly as much about the ruinous environmental, not to mention psychological, effects of wars and their devastating weapons.

However, I haven't yet given up trying. With the deepest of concerns, I ceaselessly engage with my fellow Earthlings, with the hope and conviction of doing better for ourselves and future generations.

One Planet Earth, One Human Race

We have discovered a lot about our home planet.
we now even know a lot about our universe...
but
we have not been able to keep the peace
live as civilized, thoughtful beings should live.
The "Self" which is a combination of greed,
resentment, and competition,
is still the Master.

Nasreen Pejvack

Nasreen Pejvack

HOWLING FOR LIFE

The moon facing me, gazing at me, dazzling me,
the moon and I were part of a mass,
>   within a huge ring of multitudes.
Birthing from the mass
began to shape and engage us in reactions,
>   movements of dust and rock weaved about the gloom,
>   I was born in my cradle, in a horde of entities,
the life I had was darkness, cold,
surrounded by matters I didn't know,
that was all out there,
still is.
Collisions here and there,
we expanded, shifted and moved about,
that was all out there
I desired to be what I am today
different from that mayhem,
longing to produce life, grow and transform,
darkness and cold was out there,
still is.
Eventually, clusters of us alienated from Mother Bedlam,
fell into this magnificent order,

Howling for Life

we initiated our own loop of events,
    force of our Sun shaped us,
    began a new harmonization.
    Magnum opus, the Sun, pulled and pushed us into order,
    we lined up to form, and danced riotously ever since
    we commenced a new order.
Tossed into the warmth of magnificent Sun,
gave me the heat I needed
hot and boiling to the core
I spat out blood for years, and years
torrential downpour for thousands more
only to cool it down for new life to begin
time, a drip of eternity,
yet, I was so full of hope
I desired entities that would help it grow,
they would make it more beautiful.
It took me millions of years to cultivate water,
forest, and air to breathe,
vast blue ocean nurtured the first life,
hosted all kinds of beings in its heart,
forests gave more breathing room,
became home to even more lives.
With shaking, trembling and quaking on my surface,
I developed splendid mountains.
My rivers flowed from them, joined oceans,

Nasreen Pejvack

life thrived all over my skin
and all manner of creatures helped it grow.
The birds flew about and spread seeds,
vast diverse animals grew
learning and evolving.
In due course,
        along came my evolved humanoid.
It took me a long time to enliven this ball of lava,
my resplendent chest became an absolute loveliness,
Yet
in such a brief time, my human ruined it all,
my sapiens grew to be the smartest of my children,
Yet
to have the most destructive natures.
Some of my children became the thinkers,
        learned our past mistake, thrived for change
        others developed cities, monuments,
        science fought viruses, traveled outer space
though most of my broods grew to be:
        selfish, arrogant, and clueless,
        catering to wars and conflicts.
It took me billions of years to change and re-arrange,
        give them a taste of beauty,
        breezes through singing forests,
        depth of blue sea and its vast life,

Howling for Life

peaks of mountains, and the running rivers,
so they have stories to tell, and poems to write.
Except,
ever since my children grew smarter,
they created all kinds of killing kits,
my face, my chest, my belly…
became a battle ground
dominance fell into the hands of greed,
billions of feet stamping on me,
thousands of drills piercing me,
craters in my chest,
as bombs are tossed about
destroying everything I built,
kills so many of my children,
destroys my vegetation,
they began a chain of destruction of all,
greeneries, life in my oceans
extracting any treasures in my belly
anything to feed their egos
and I thought they are the smartest of all my beings,
my little humanoid, the sapiens.

Question yourself my children,
do you think you are blameless?

Nasreen Pejvack

>Some of you err by deliberate choices,
>some are weak or ignorant or cynical,
>some only value their own ideas,
>some are the idols of greed in the temples,
>some thrive with adventurous souls, for change.

Though are not united,
they have segmented me with many borders
borders created wars and hatreds
fighting for a bigger piece of me
killing for land to increase wealth
As treasures found in my heart,
my surface, my other creations
plunged into the abyss of suffering,
more greed, thereafter, more wars
even wars about who is better.

If I am the mother of all, I remember well,
>amongst my creatures, those who roam my forests,
>climb my mountains and pass through my oceans,
>fly across and around me,

I only sprouted one human race.
Yet
some think they are different and superior,
aren't they oblivious to their own ignorance?

Though, I believe in some of my humans,

Howling for Life

the ones that know the mistakes made,
the ones who want change, and know how to change,
Yet, the struggle is too hard.
Remember my children:
I have given life,
I rained-down on my bare hot surface,
flourished life, made it possible to grow,
I gave you all you needed,
But
all is evaporating in madness, darkness,
hunger and wars you have created,
pain and suffering you brought upon each other,
Yet,
none see their own fault,
none see they are the cause of such problems.
Well my children:
the moon still faces me, gazing at me, dazzling me
I am still part of the same mass
I was a lava rock, I will survive
I will surely grow life again and flourish my bare chest once more,
But the question is
Will you be there?

Nasreen Pejvack

WAITING

I am daughter of Gaia
        mother earth weeps
I am tears of the mountains, joining rivers
        together we join oceans
I am lover of earth's forests, oceans and mountains
        Raven flaps silently
I have climbed hard mountains, seeking freedom,
        hearing liberty
I have traveled across the world, seeking liberation,
        talking of freedom
I have followed our thinkers, listened to speeches,
        seeking a liberated world
I long for peace on mother earth
        still I am waiting
I dream of a united world, no war, no slaughter
        yet hopelessly only wishing it, not tasting it

I still climb mountains, roam forests,
        enjoy birds, and talk of love.

Yet those around me are oblivious to the real me;

Howling for Life

    the real me is bleeding,

you are the power behind me, next to me
you are the one who shares this world with me
you are making it grow and develop
you can contribute to its happiness
you can make a difference or be indifferent

Have I given up hope
    Not yet
Have I waited too long
    Undeniably
Have I lost my trust
    Not yet
Have I wished for us to make it right
    Indeed

Nasreen Pejvack

FACES OF WAR

1

I love biking these paths,
alongside Fraser River
  tranquil woods, sparkling cheerful birds
  chickadees, sparrows, robins
  they fly right through me, my bike
  cheerfully sing, dance, eat
and there is this kind woman,
  sitting by the river
  feeds crows, pigeons and seagulls
they gather around her, eat from her hands
eating together, sharing seeds.

Breeze mingles with my sigh
birds in lands of struggle, clash
  surely flee to holes,
  seek shelter, safe places
  little boys and girls too
  men and women, search for shelter
all creatures run from rockets, bombs and death.

Faces of War

Is there a safe place for them all?
As for us, relaxed, carefree ones in safe lands
ignorance, unawareness, silence, kills just like any weapon.

Nasreen Pejvack

2

Face down on a beach, chilly water
    a little human, a little boy
    was loved and nurtured
    he lays lifeless, face down
    his life has been robbed
    too short, gone, so soon
    who is answering for his death
    carnage all around, who is plotting
they blame it on one another,
blame extremist, fanatic
war lord, fundamentalist, intruder, imposter

No, let's blame damned black gold,
diamond, iron-ore, uranium blemish
those lands that hold rich resources
for all those treasures, people bleeding
blood is drawn elsewhere
who plot it all
do not care for life
play blameless, innocent
who manufacture pain, displacement
which creates more angry masses
as for us, relaxed, carefree ones in safe lands
ignorance, unawareness, silence, kills just like any weapon.

Faces of War

3

Hungry, cold, running for shelters
      running for dear life
      running for a better life
      running for their children
      running in opposition to madness
but where to?
who to?
In safe lands:
many are scared of them
many call them ignorant, religious
aloof, ill-mannered

No? You don't want them?
why so many wars
who benefits from wars
how to stop wars
when will we act against wars

As for us, relaxed, carefree ones in safe lands
ignorance, unawareness, silence, kills just like any weapon.

Nasreen Pejvack

4

War for commodities
It's Black Friday once again
next Boxing Day sale
ah, maybe deep discounts for Valentine's Day
perhaps Apple has released a new gadget
wow, look at those ravenous line-ups for the latest device
      destined to be obsolete within a year.

While we are busy in those lines
      Wherever they happen
masters are ransacking the world's resources
conceivable, in any bloody way
fuel madness, feed their ravenousness

lands with resources are bleeding
blood is drawn elsewhere

And while we are looking for more bargains
in our safe heavens,
ignorance, unawareness, silence, kills just like any weapon.

5

Wars mingling the blood
blood of all hemispheres
Africa, Middle East
    With Europe
men bleed
blood of men of all colours
    is red
    pain feels the same
    heart beat, homesickness, love of family
    confusion
is all the same
as war, is only a gigantic chaos and confusion for us
    wealth and control for war architects

Nasreen Pejvack

Eternal Remembrance Day

Philosophers, writers, legends
have long impeached us on our bloody battles
        the man-made wars for profits
Pain on our earth and its lovely creatures
      and to each other
what have we learned
      we sure learned, learned to dedicate a day,
      for the fallen soldiers
      to remember them
how about an alternative
      Stop the madness
      Seek a way to dispute without arms

Decades ago a war blasted our home
      many suffered, horribly died
we assigned a day to remember
      Lest we forget
      November 11, for fallen soldiers,
killed for nothing,
people in ditches, cold, hungry,
waiting days for orders to come.

The unknown ones,

Ordered to kill, men they never knew,
who never harmed them,
did not even speak the same language,
Did not know why they were fighting,
An order, obedience and misplaced faith,
I feel for both, hunter and hunted,
It wasn't their war, but their commands,
nonetheless,
we have a remembrance day
to celebrate their lives
honoring their unfair, unnecessary deaths
A new war created yearly
killing continues
we have a day assigned
Killings continue for later commemoration
men kill men they do not know
fear, follow orders
an eternal Remembrance Day

Nasreen Pejvack

BEYOND CONTROL

Cycle, force of nature
happens while resting, in the dark of night
>   takes me in my sleep
>   midst of a busy day
>   makes one run for dear life

land moves beneath me
>   everything collapses,

storms and thunders wash cities
>   with people

volcano flow red rivers, all
Beyond any control,
no one is ready
no one foresee
>   destroy cities
>   take lives.

We went to the moon,
found distant galaxies, far-flung worlds
cured ills and managed plagues
built towers to the skies
tested nuclear, shattered two cities
wiped out souls
praised the bomber.

If money spent on machines of death
was used to study quakes and storms
we could have mastered the signs
made time to plan or flee

But it happens and happens
      all the world over
         takes lives by thousands
            orphans children
then comes the predator,
      takes what he can
         chaos reigns
people watch at 6 o'clock
follow a while, soon all forget,
life goes on.

If we gave ample care, study and learn
so many lives could be saved
one less thing we'd have to fear

Nasreen Pejvack

REMEMBERING SPARTACUS

I remember Spartacus:
I remember him, yearning for his distant home
    but he won't know where home is
Remembers its smell
    a soft and kind voice
    all he recalls from childhood
    faraway land…

I remember Spartacus
    Sees himself human,
    Won't fight at the slavemaster's command
    Won't give in to bloody battle
    Pities the numb crowd that enjoys the spectacle of pain

Rome created a masterpiece of diversion
offering carnage
    I remember many fallen Spartacuses
    Who fought for truth

I remember them
    Walking, talking, laughing with wounded hearts,
    dreaming of home

Today, we mock Rome's Colosseum,
call it but a showcase for slaughter
have matured in our art and science
       but have we bent the knees of aggression
       have you seen Spartacuses

No, today, aided by art and science
we have colosseums of cinema and video games
       home entertainment

Not in Rome, but in our home,
       watch butchery and suffering.
Today, art and science create mass attractions
works like a charm
       effect
hardened indifferent masses.

Today, we view news with distant killings,
flicks with synthetic massacres
       Ahh, dear Spartacus
we still kill, still encourage it,
watch how one dominates another
       honorable killers,
       wreaking havoc from afar,
give awards to those who best formulate death

Nasreen Pejvack

we encourage murder today
count the ways, name the ways
      and I
I look in vain, does any Spartacus remain

LAW OF THE JUNGLE

Green fields, grazing pasture,
Singing wind, dancing trees
Playful newborn deer, worried mother

Middle of forest, tiger watches
    Cubs need food
one with cubs, one goes hunting,

Buck sees him, runs to distract,
Tiger chases, buck loses,
Tiger holds him down, his eyes say
    I want to live,
    I have my family to care for.
Survival, doe moves along, with her fawns
    Tigers and cubs,
    Full tummy
Law of jungle, survival of species.
    ***
Kids are playing in their alley,
cheerful, laughing, chasing their ball
no mother to watch them, it is their alley
Bomb drops, children vanish

Nasreen Pejvack
Why
Law of jungle
Middle of city
In their own alley
On their own planet
Where there is room for all of us…

who did not want them
who allows mass killing
who caters to war and destruction

Why do we put up with it
     knowing the bullies
     knowing the reasons

Ah, I remember, they direct resources
     bullies kill,
     consumers watch,
Enduring that law of jungle
     maintain distractions
     blissful consumers

ONE UNIFIED EARTH

We need one another, find me, unite
together, we will be one, strong and unified

Let me find you, let us become whole, unite
in peace, one world, no borders, unified

Where there are no borders there are no wars
when there are no wars, people are unified

With no wars, children sleep in peace
their rulers and caretakers are unified

Children are not hungry, they go to school
they do not have fear, they are unified

One earth, one human race
Unified

Nasreen Pejvack

Women
Vital essence of life
Embryo of our future
Foundation of existence
Woman, mother, daughter, sister
Eradicate them
and there is nothing

WOMEN

1

Women
The vital essence of life
The embryo of the future
The foundation of existence
Woman, mother, daughter and sister
Eradicate them, and there is nothing

There was a day when silence encircled them
A day when
    if she wrote a poem,
    it was under a man's name
    if she sang a song or acted
        she was unrefined
            molested
    if she pursued sport
        she was wild and foolish,
  ill-treated
Her fate was chosen,
by father, husband, brother
could she be a doctor, lawyer, judge?
Her capacities were doctored, lawyered and judged

Nasreen Pejvack

Who made that resolve? Men?
>	We voted out that archaic nonsense
>	We reveal our strength
>	We enlarge science, literature and history
>	We sweep away the ancient axioms
>	We create men, give birth to them
>	but we have raised them poorly
>	forgotten the most important lessons
>	flawed arrogant sons

We give them life to be our partners,
>	but some turn against us
>	consider us emotional, illogical

Our faults are plain
>	we failed in solidarity
>>		did not teach you well

We love you at birth and as you grow
>	bring you to flourish
>	Don't teach power and destruction
>	Don't teach slaughter,
>>		belief in demagogues

No, we nourish you
take care of you
>	If you are wounded or lost

Women

We do not give birth to soldiers, to fighters
    We give to our world, humans born to no caste
    We are your mothers, sisters and lovers,
But above all, we are your equal.

Nasreen Pejvack
2

We never choose a religion
>we were forced to it,
>kindly and lovingly.
>Muslim, Christian, Jewish, Hindu, Buddhist
>Is there more
We were born to one
shadow the same blind practice
we raise our children to one
>with no question asked.

Women
Let's stop shaping our children
Let them choose
Let them see
Let them read our history
>that all religions killed just the same
each justifies carnage
But
had slaughtered just the same
behave, just the same
If I don't believe in one
>then I am the enemy

but am I

Women

No, I am just a free-spirited woman
who doesn't like to be told
who loves to learn and choose
That is all

Nasreen Pejvack

3

Women
      have we talked
      discussed and reasoned
Let's see
if women were ruling the world
      would we have as many conflicts
      wars
      sick competitions
No!
After all science has proven
We are the wise ones!
      stronger ones
      most caring, reliable
      brave ones
Let's prove it,
with us in power
there will be a safer world
      Are you up to it?
Let's go

Women

4

Sisterhood, Motherhood
you are the daughter I never had
darling you are my sister, from another mother
I cannot trust anyone but you
But
it all falls into a blackhole
if one doesn't play as one wishes
    doesn't share the same opinion
    has a new idea
    is strong minded, a fighter
Then, all is forgotten

we are sisters to joy and to sorrow
link rivers to oceans
channels and mirror the poles
    through the sky
women the divine messengers
passing through, from all colours
    key to a successful sisterhood,
unification, acceptance, reverence,
    if we don't have that
then we are men

Nasreen Pejvack

5

She is a cricket
      who chirps in the field
           spreads love and devotions
though the storm comes along
rain falls in torrents,
drowning
although as soon as deluge is clear
the cricket, the little musician
      undaunted, resumes
           with another song
                with glory of enchantment
delightfully binges on the seeds

LOVE AND INSPIRATION

Mother says, you are so pretty
      but, she looks at her askance,
Mother says, oh, you are taller than me
      with a subtle anxious tone

Neighbour says to her
      your daughter is so elegant and brilliant
Mother says, oh, yes
      I am so proud of her
           but she fumes and sends her home
Her head down on the way
thinking
      she loves me or she hates me
      always gloomy
      I would never be like mother
      women must help each other
      to advance
      not to depress
Thinking
      "I would never be like her"
other children are irritated
      angry at each other, and everyone,

Nasreen Pejvack

why is that
    how many mothers disappoint as mothers
    what was her story
Am I seeing another reason
    for this disarray of disheartened people
how many like her cannot teach love
maybe she never learned,
she competes with her sister just the same

Perhaps I will know better someday,
    when I am older

I Choose

Lonely nights, dark room, hiding
lock the door, feel safe, look up
      stars shining
Breathing light, fears at rest
looking at stars, wondering
      are there any planets around those shining points of light
      is there a lonely terrified girl up there
      is she sitting at her window looking for me
      is she as scared as I.
On that far away planet
      perhaps they do not damage their children
      perhaps they do not decide for the girls
      perhaps they love their girls,
            just as much as their boys
      perhaps they are all happy

Crickets chirping, a clamour she loves
Crickets sing. Together. Loud.
      Crickets block vulgar sounds, anger.

Morning comes, tired, sleepless
      school is joy, away from home
      school makes her forget

Nasreen Pejvack

Night arrives
    long, lonely and dark
    dark room, lock the door, stars twinkle
    breathing shallowly, fears at rest
    gazing at stars, hoping for salvation, rescue.
Inside voice screaming
    Only I can liberate the human inside me
    Only I can make the necessary changes
    Only I will be the judge of my life

Perhaps I am young for the journey
    Yet I am strong and smart
Journey will be tough
    sea will be rough
    continents far apart
    people strange, landscapes striking
        Time will tell

INTELLIGENT SPECIES

has touched the sky, our universe
has speared around the seed of knowledge
also, wars destroy all
      crude humans
where is the intelligence
war follows us throughout history
      as boys love their toys
      wealth made from those bloody toys
I am a woman
      the blood of history
      voice of future
      author, designer of life
for my imminent cohort
just to flourish and keep our home for all

men barricade walls
for comfortable illusions of control

Berlin's wall crumbled
      Jerusalem's went up
            Planning for the Mexican one

Nasreen Pejvack

Where has the intelligent species gone
nothing makes sense,
women ache for peace

Intelligence searches for unity
      Won't allow wars to follow

I indulge my garden
Encourage my flowers to flourish
I nurture life
They thrive
I give back to Mother Earth
Hurry, hurry little garden
Expand, enlarge, be tall and proud
Give life

Nasreen Pejvack

My Garden, My Sanctuary

Melancholy, frustration,
      hindrance, burden
then, I seek out my garden
      indulge it tenderly
        encourage my flowers to flourish swiftly
        nurture the herbs lovingly
        care for a place that gives life
thus, my sanctuary, my redeemer
      where, for a small while,
        I can forget the madness of mankind
        destructiveness of self

There, I breathe calmly, inhale life, gather energy
      rejuvenate to challenge the foolishness out there

My garden, My sanctuary

SPRING ALWAYS ARRIVES

Tall mountains surround old villages
snow covered pastures, farms
short days, long nights, cold and dark
hungry wolves howl
        hunt for prey.
Not much to do in daylight hours
bodies rest during languid nights
warm fire, wine and poetry
stories and songs
love and life
tellers of tales improvise
singers sing
Joyous sounds drown out wailing winds and howling wolves.

Stories of last year's events
        who fell in love
        who was married
        who has a new baby
        who started another war
And there are the old stories
        legends, passed down
        generation to generation

Nasreen Pejvack

Children play, laugh, then fall into mothers' arms

Dark cold, winter passes,
      life is born again, spring arrives
      blossoms everywhere,
      smell new life
      so much of life in spring
      Pastures are green, buds all around
      children running
      mothers, fathers working hard
      cultivating farms,
      re-arranging, harvesting,
All the while, creating new stories for the next long, chilly winter nights

IN A DAY

Sun rising,
a new day,
Wide open ocean, endless emerald vistas
     golden sun, shimmering water
     offering a day brimful of life.

Foggy ocean, lonely bird, tranquil water
sun and ocean; horizons of hope and serenity
     I stroll along the beach
     captivated by the day, brimful of life.

Ritual dance of light and water
creates supreme colours,
my heart bleeds into my hands, nostalgia
     leap back
     beauty of the day, brimful of life.

Hearing the moving crowd, opening the day
striving for comforts, competing
     missing the day, brimful of life.

Stressful day, pushing and pulling us
we have lost harmony, the meaning of life

Nasreen Pejvack

we do not know how to immerse ourselves
      in the awe-inspiring sunrise or sunset
      in a day, so brimful of life.
Luminous, immaculate sundown
I stroll along the beach, going back
soaking in the mystical surroundings
      probing the day and its beauty, thinking

Did I get enough of it
After all,
      I am now one day older

SPARROW

Sparrows in the backyard,
chestnut sparrow, savannah and lark sparrow,
    is it a sparrow's convention?
This year many of them visit
    even a bee hummingbird
    chirping, soaring, dancing
    eating,
But I did not put out any seeds,
    one flies up and disappears
    returns with ten more birds
    inviting others to the symposium

Ah, I know, my bad back this year
    I did not cut the deadheads
        this year
    garden must have an abundance of seeds
        this year
If fallen seeds and a cluttered yard,
    brings me that many happy cheerful lives
    I will surely plan a muddled yard
    with even more hidden seeds
    next year

Nasreen Pejvack

So much energy, increase daily
      as if they tell one another

They come to eat and dance, play and drink
      when they leave
I find myself waiting for them the next day,
      my free and happy birds

SHARE

Crow, flying, gliding
 searching for food
houses as far as eyes can see
cars and objects
People, black, blond and red heads
—and their garbage

Bear comes out of hibernation with her cubs
    hungry, looking for food
        all she sees fences and roads
        fill the landscape
        aggressive people
— and their garbage

Sea creatures tangled up
        in human waste, toxins

Advanced techno-toys
        our obsessions
        oblivious to consequences
we seize and conquer everything

Nasreen Pejvack

Dew

Early morning dew,
leaves and flowers
      I used to search for it,
        would look to see which of my flowers had more
      I loved to touch, feel, taste, the morning dew

What has changed my love for it
      I don't see it anymore,
        seek it no more,
not because there is no more
but because of tears
      dew-like on the cheeks of hungry
      scared, displaced children
blinds me to other kind

Am I not romantic anymore
have I become insensitive
      No, I am only awed by
      tear-stained cheeks of earth's children,
      dew-like

I do talk of love, only poles apart
I love a world without war and suffering
happiness for all
joyful eyes, not teary ones
a united world

Nasreen Pejvack

I Do Talk of Love!

They tell me I don't write about love
that I don't write about rosy cheeks, striking men
but about wars, anguish and devastation
that I only see the suffering of Earth
that I should see the beauty of it

Write of love, love making, affection
      write of happiness and beautiful colourful meadows
         write of his hair, her eyes

I cry out
I do talk of love, only poles apart
a world without war and suffering
      filled with happiness for all
      joyful eyes, not teary ones
      a united world with no war
           filled with love

I long for the haves to let the have-nots keep their
      possessions, wealth and resources
      peace for everyone
      world with no bigotry

I Do Talk of Love!

Then I can talk of love
see, I do talk of love, and write of love
only differently

If there is no war
we will all be happy, enamoured, rosy cheeked
we will all talk about passion, love making
      we will all have peace
      insights, intuitions,

How can I talk of rosy cheeks and beautiful eyes
      when there are so many bloody cheeks and teary eyes

When we all love each other,
      as one nation
            I will be ecstatic,
That day we all can talk of love

Nasreen Pejvack

I LOVE A MAN

I met this man, who is old enough to have a family,
although he lives alone, loves his solitude,
    he is kind, giving
    understanding, loving,
    open-minded, accepting

He read and learned like an old chum I knew a long time ago,
    humbly, though sadly observes mankind,
we don't speak the same language,
    have the same culture,
    but we talked for hours as if
    we knew each other for centuries

He was so easy to talk to, still is.
I asked, with all that wonderful nature
    why he is alone,
        I haven't fallen in love yet,
        smiling

Shiver on my back, I thought,
    I have heard that sentiment before.

I Love a Man

I stared at him,
>I am falling for you, he said
>>then you are in trouble,
>I sense that, he said

He could see right through me
>my vulnerable being, the fears

You must be patient, I said
>I already am

Decades passed, I have loved him since then,
I now know,
>it is thrilling to be a woman…
>learn, create, be a freedom fighter,
>adventurous and
>>to love a man with passion

Nasreen Pejvack

MY OTHER HALF

The dark night moves quickly
    if I am with you
        days are brighter
            when I am with you
                meadows look greener,
                    when I am with you
Our house, Filled with laughter
when we are together!

homesickness fades away
    when you talk of love
loneliness flies away
            when you whisper songs of love
Though it rains, my heart shines, because you are here
our house, filled with laughter
When we are together!

Ahh, our moments, our life of decades,
matching spirits shared
similar sceneries loved
two bodies, one spirit
is that the true meaning of

My Other Half

"my other half"
We really are of the same kind,
the affinity is so vivid, so strong,
we smile at one another
with lips, and with eyes,
smiles, overflowing
With joy and promises!

Nasreen Pejvack

Delineate Love

1

Hearing pensive sounds of Piano
      island of memories, glides in
      nostalgic thoughts
remembering his innocent, loving eyes
fearfully saying
      I love you, as life
      won't survive without the warmth of the sun
That his days
      are brighter and most beautiful beside you
      seeing you makes his heart smile
      his life is complete
That
      her smile makes his day shine
      her voice is the sounds of nature
      breathing is difficult
      if he doesn't see her in a day.

Piano Playing
      ages of memories
      beat of life, moving her ahead

Delineate Love

    his warm devoted voice
    mingles with piano's tone
as she remembers his velvety voice asking
    to be his life-long partner
    his eternal love, his comrade
for ever, and ever

Piano's melody reflecting his voice
    Let's breathe together,
    laugh together and share a life together

his words, his voice
contemplating with song
remembering his agitated face
    his concerned arguments

Do you even love me

Chopin's nocturn fills the room
    cries blend with the song
    howling,
    I did love you
    I will always love you
I didn't know how to say it
    Did not know
how to be a woman
I didn't know

Nasreen Pejvack

2

Island of memories raises
        above the river of life
        walking alongside river
listening to motion of water
            moving along
        recite a poem, murmuring with babbling river
        I do love you,
          with the heights of love for humanity,
             with the warmth of sun, and all joys in life,
                with deepest love for a brother, a
comrade, a lover, if I knew

Alongside you it is so easy
        fighting against obtuseness,
we will arrive at our freedom together,
        with our people,
        what a great victory, that could be

Someday we will watch the sunrise
        without fear of arrest,
and watch the sundown
        with joy of liberty
        we are freedom-fighters,

Delineate Love

    we should only think of our purpose,
why do you want to destroy us - with mortal love
we love each other for a greater aspiration,
    I love you as a brother,
        a comrade, a freedom-fighter
I love to fight alongside you to bring knowledge,
    awareness,
Freedom has become a dream for all of us
Let's see it together
    taste it together
The love you are offering is strange to me

Sits at the water,
Feet feels the coolness,
    water brushes with memories
        shimmering with rays of light
            feet in water, head on fold knees
I should have told him
I have changed, I feel him
I see him, conversely
    I see the way he looked at me
        noticed occasionally he smelled my hair
            I felt his strong emotions
I should have told him
I see your sizzling tears when you watch me

Nasreen Pejvack

    gives me shivers
    I do not know why
    but I like the feeling.

Birds are chirping
Soaring, following one another tree to tree
they sing as reminiscences fly with them
remembering
    his fingers play my favorite songs only
        he only read my choice of poems
            oh, my dearest,
              how much I wanted to know,
              feel that love all over him.
      The same as him.
Birds, whispering water,
    circulates with her cry
    I wanted you to teach me,
    teach me to be a woman
        with all her feelings
    I did not understand passionate love,
        I dreaded it
    With your love, wash away my fear,
    With your poems, bring out the feeling of a woman,
    With your kind look wash away the distrust,
    With your music clear my mind,
Tell me how to love you…

Delineate Love

Our work would improve if we were one.

      I wanted to try that
      I wanted to be complete
      I wanted you to teach me, how to love a man

Decades have passed, my darling
I am still wandering like a gypsy
      roaming forests, with roaring wind
      climbing mountains, with their snags
      watching eagles proudly fly
gloomy, travel around wondering,
scribbling notes, poems
questioning what would happen
what would be out there if, only if
      I would feel what you felt
      were we together today

Nasreen Pejvack

3

Time passes, memories alive
      dream faithfully
I want to pin my dreams
touch him, though
      he is not there
           he is nowhere
demon hands took him away
evil killed a superior human
they will never know his depths
his deep love for humanity
      one who could even rationalize,
           why a torturer tortures.
They shed his blood
never knew his meaning.

Forgive me my love
      forgive me for not understanding
           forgive me that you never knew
                how much I loved you
                    I never knew
Vulgar ignorance conquered
People watched the murderers
      I ran away from the criminal hands of religion
      from the hell of ignorance

Delineate Love

from people who watched - murderers
People who did not understand
do not understand
true meaning of love, devotion
      continue living with demons
and I confess
I am living with memories
      sweet memories, vivid dreams,
           treasures of joy and sorrow

Acknowledgment

Versions of a few of these poems have been published in two Anthology collections. Two have appeared on Inanna Publication's blog and my own website.

This book is for all those who diligently and actively work to end chaos and bring order and peace to this world.

AUTHOR BIOGRAPHY

Nasreen Pejvack is a published author, with her novel "Amity" published by Inanna Pubs, York University Press in October of 2015. Soon after, it was shortlisted for BC's 2016 Ethel Wilson Book Prize.

She left Iran a few years after the 1979 revolution. She lived in Athens for several months, and then left Greece for Canada to begin a new life in a more peaceful environment. In Ottawa she studied computer programming at Algonquin College and worked in the field for over 11 years (Programmer, Application Developer). She then moved to California to work as a Systems Analyst/Project Manager for CNet during the tech boom of the 1990s.

After several years she returned to her new homeland of Canada and BC, where she left the IT field and decided to start a new chapter in her life, studying and working as a counselor and educator, while pursuing a degree in Psychology.

Following her successful novel Amity, she is now here presenting short tales inspired by her experiences of life in Canada.

Nasreen Pejvack

Nasreen's other hobby is the research, design, development and presentation of a variety of workshops on various aspects of our society. Her book of poetry "Waiting" was published at the same time as her collection of short tales "Paradise of Downcast," both of which were published in 2018.

Nasreen was a judge for the 2018 BC Ethel Wilson Fiction Prize. Also, President of Royal City Literary Arts Society since May 2016.

https://www.examine-consider-act.ca/

www.ingramcontent.com/pod-product-compliance
Lightning Source LLC
Chambersburg PA
CBHW030916080526
44589CB00010B/326